GW01326646

Everyday Prayers

Illustrations by Maureen Bradley

A LITTLE LION

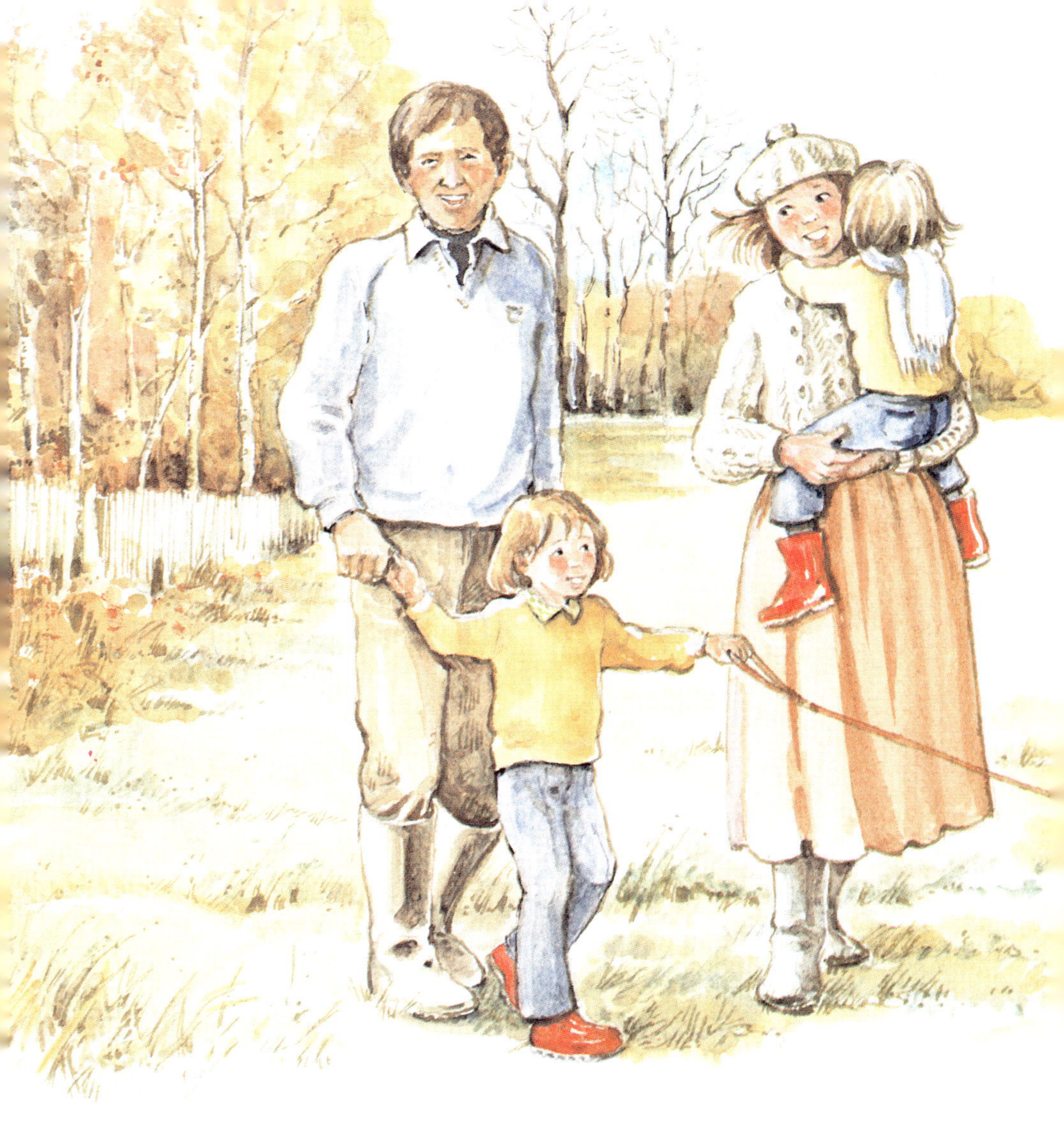

Today

This is the day
that God has made.
We will rejoice
and be glad in it.

Father, we thank you

Father, we thank you for the night,
And for the pleasant morning light;
For rest and food and loving care,
And all that makes the day so fair.
Help us to do the things we should,
To be to others kind and good;
In all we do at work or play
To grow more loving every day.

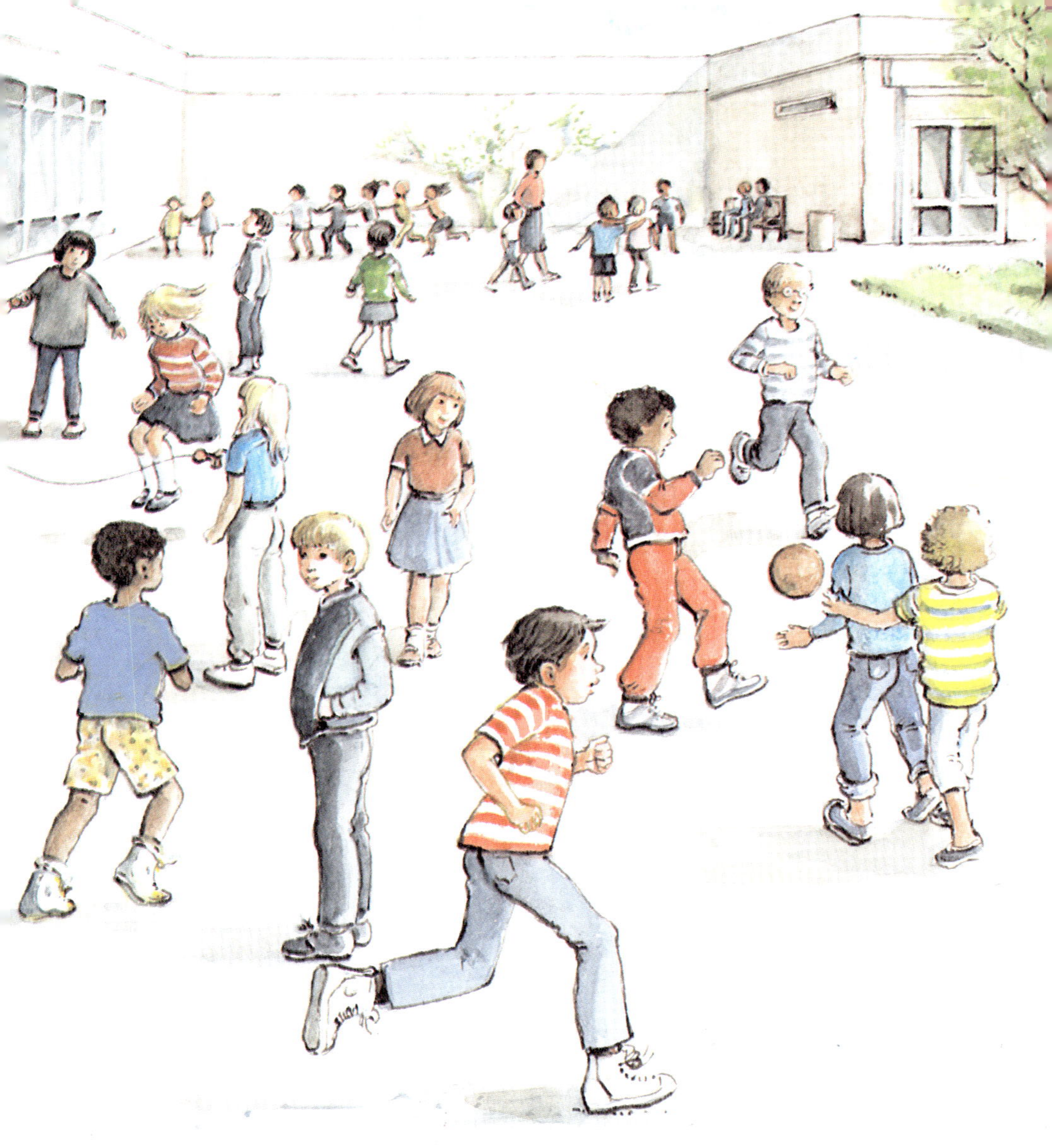

In the morning

Heavenly Father,
you have given this new day to me.
Help me to make it one that pleases you
by doing my best in everything,
because I love you.

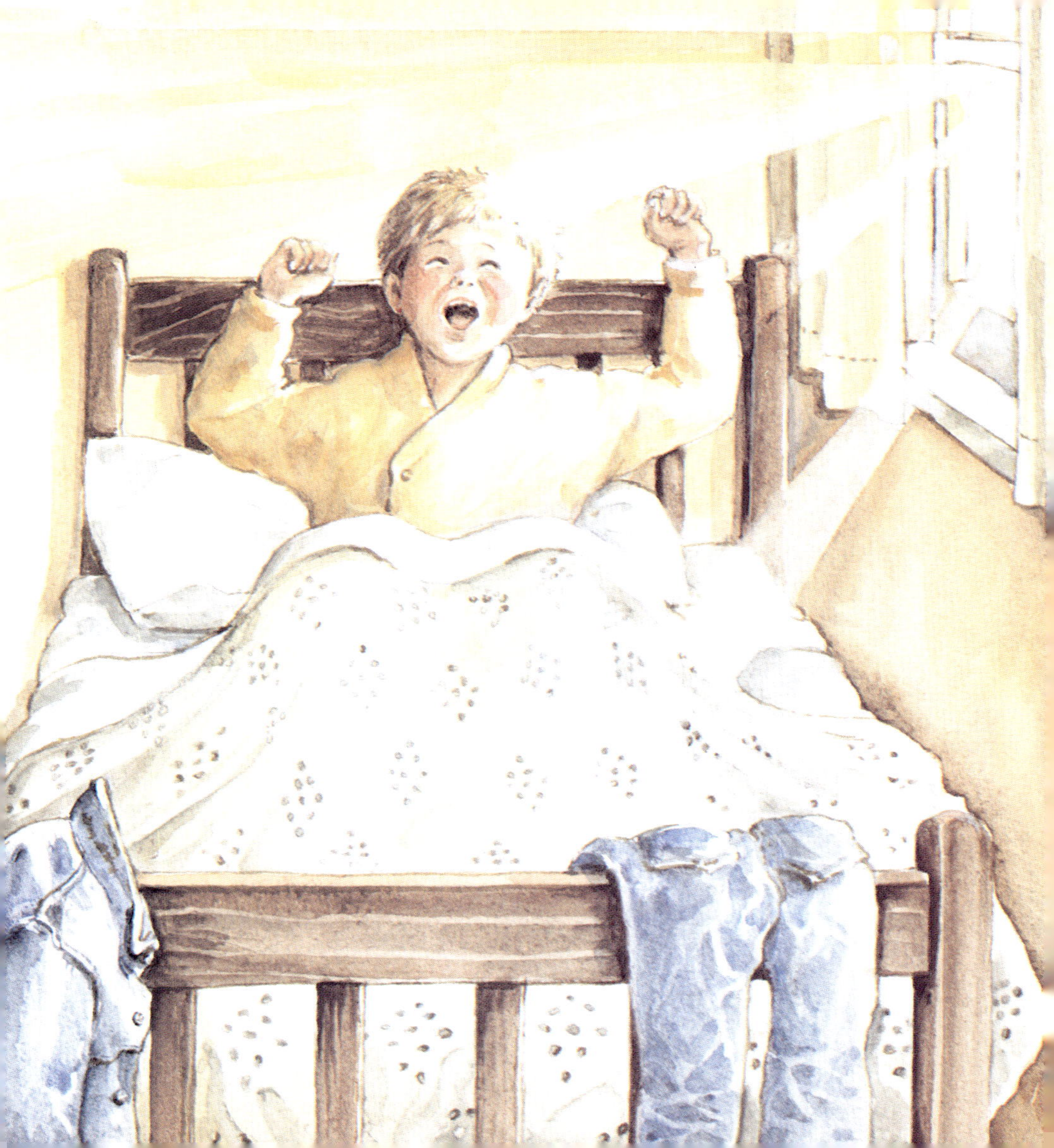

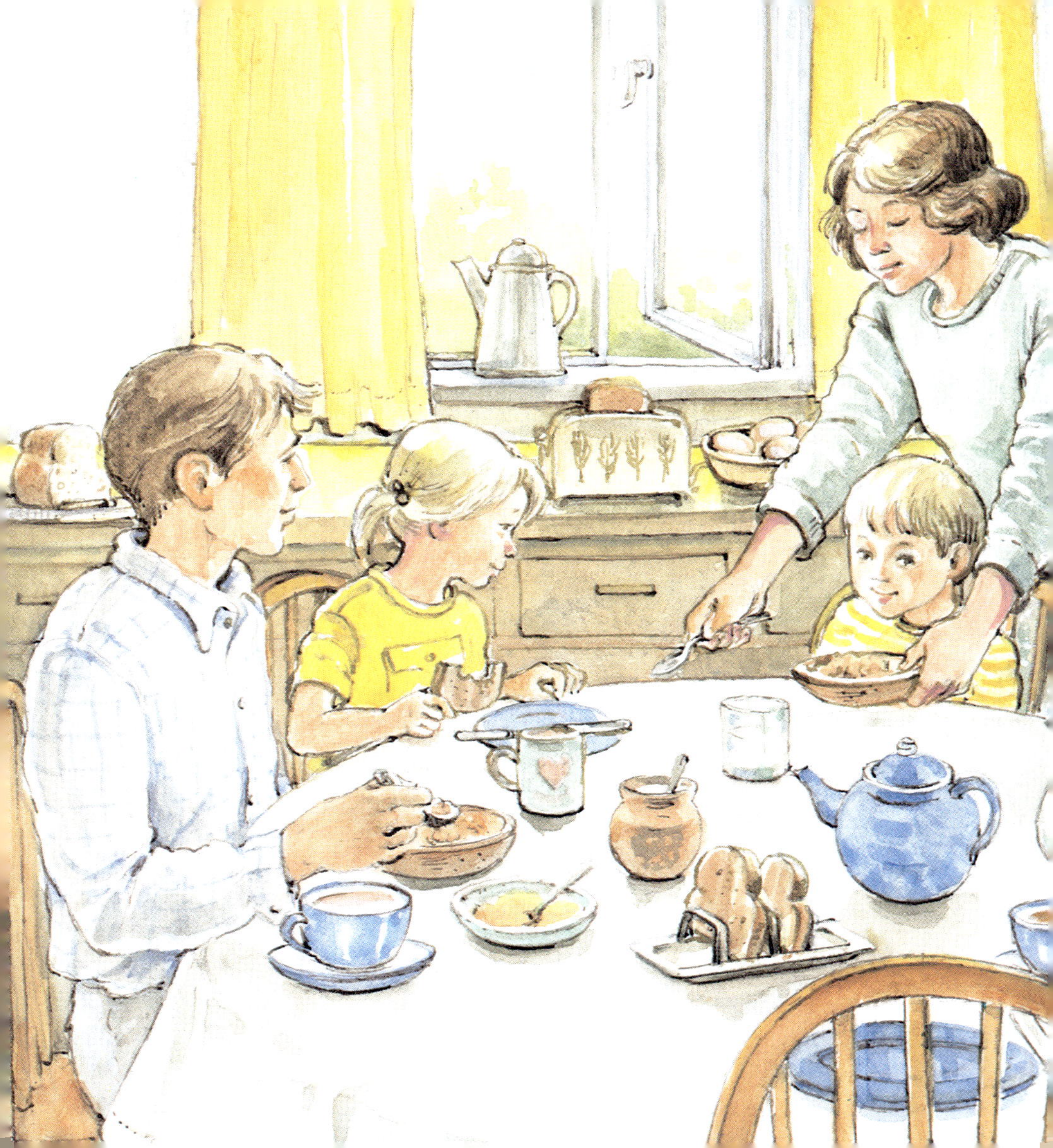

Thank you

For this new morning with its light,
Father, I thank you.
For rest and shelter of the night,
Father, I thank you;
For health and food,
for love and friends
for everything your goodness sends,
Father in heaven, I thank you.

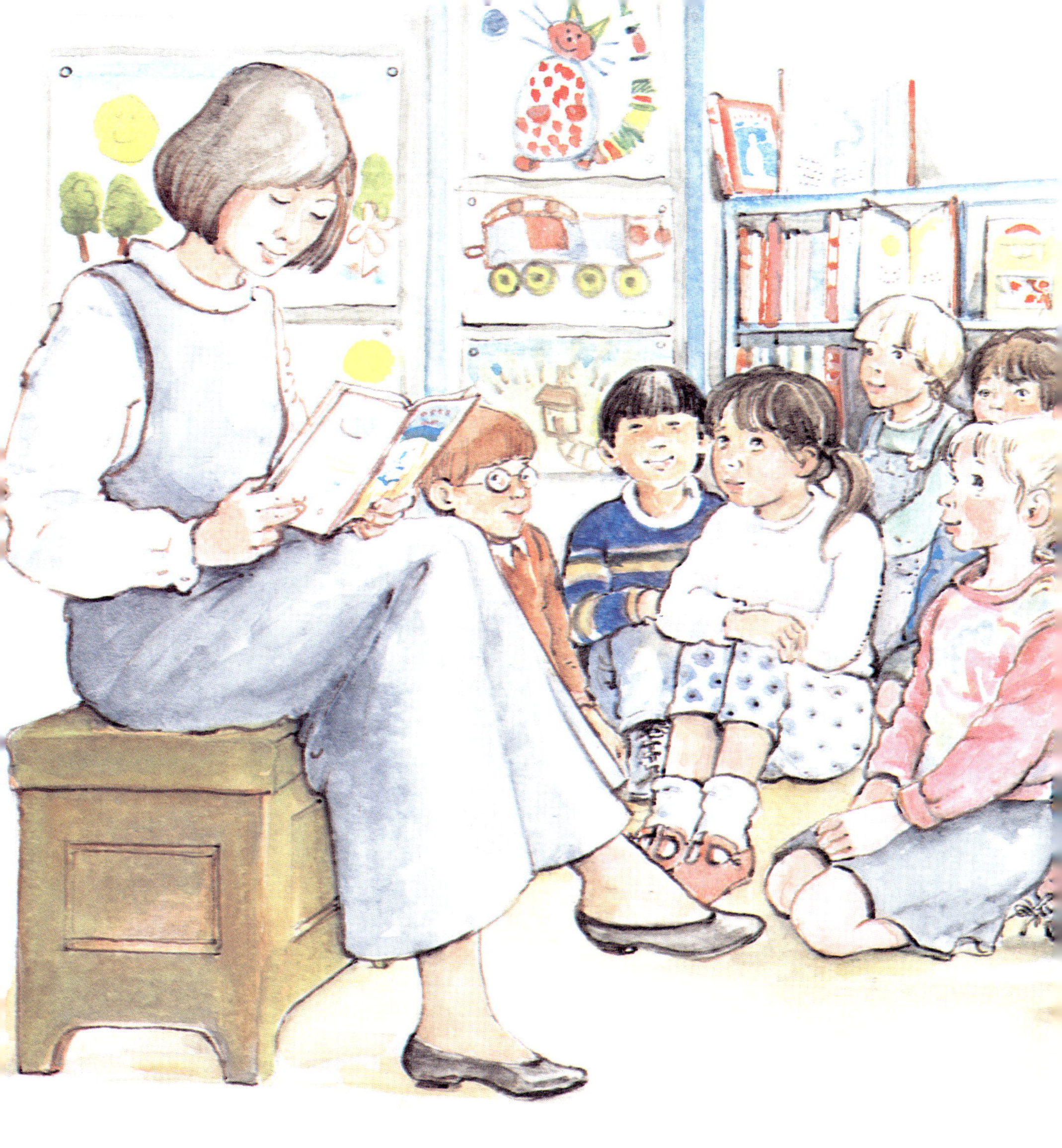

At school

Thank you, God, for this new day
In my school to work and play.
Please be with me all day long,
In every story, game and song.
May all the happy things we do
Make you, our Father, happy too.

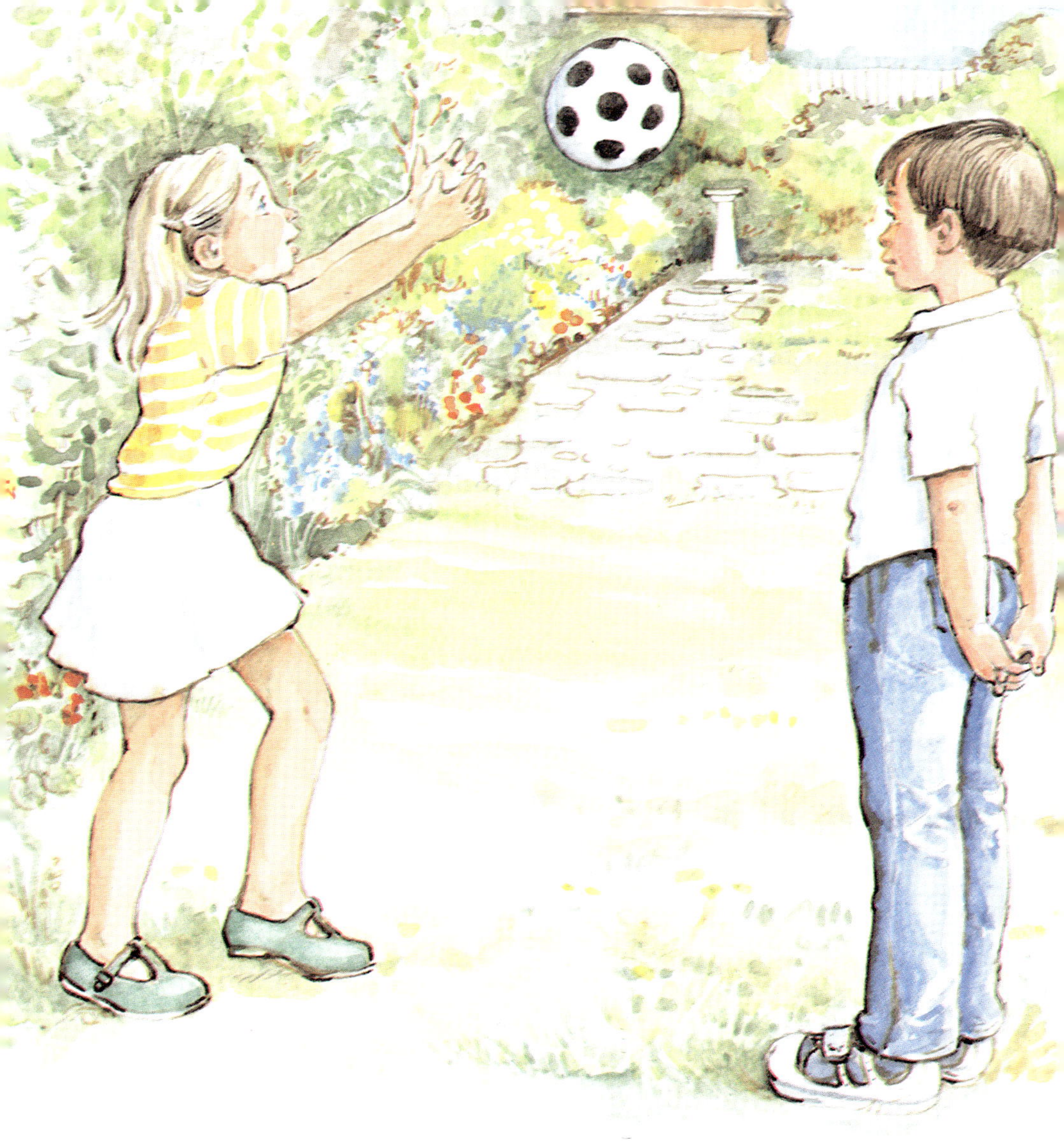

A happy day

Loving Father, on this day
Make us happy in our play,
Kind and helpful, playing fair,
Letting others have a share.

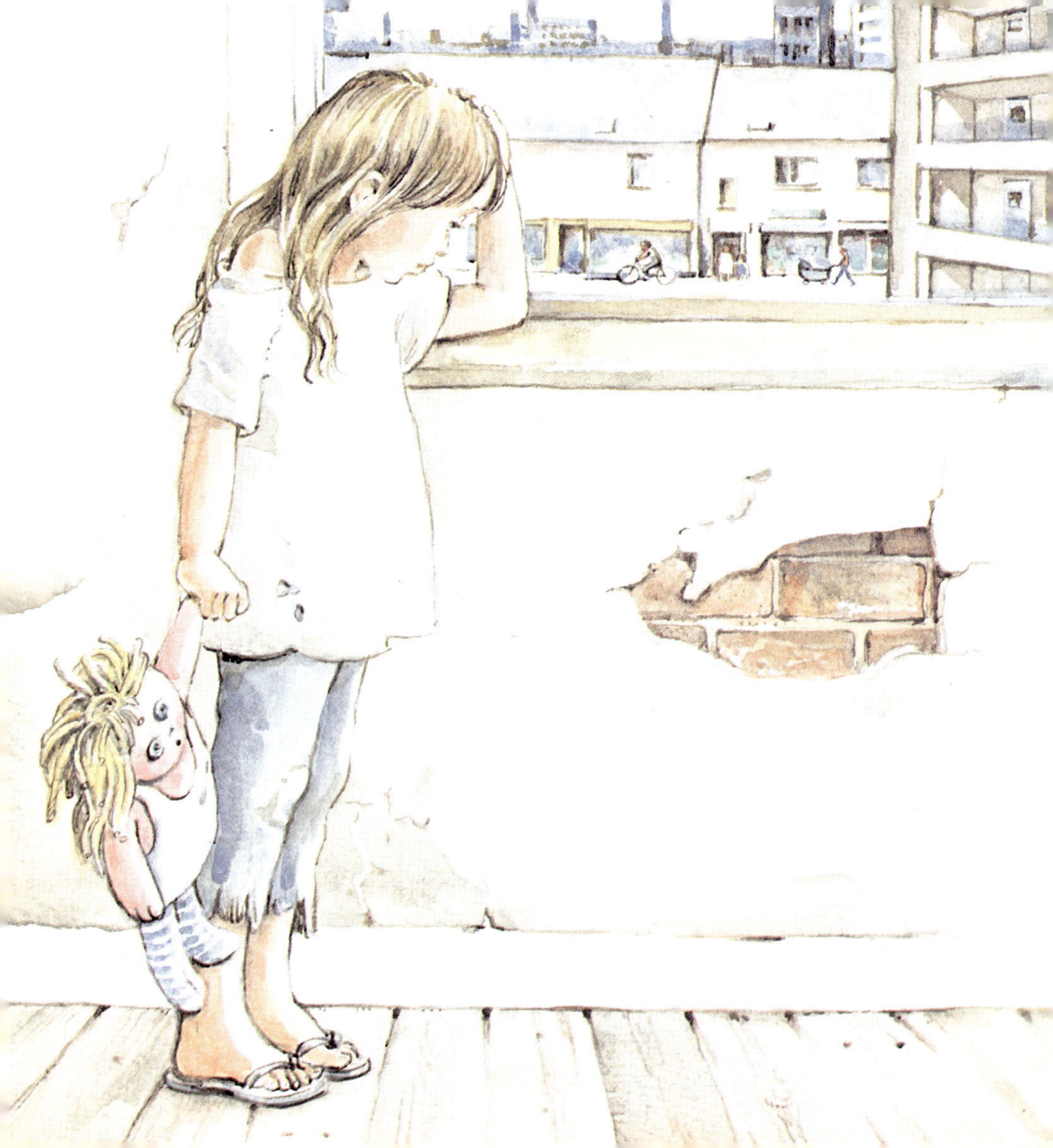

For those who suffer

Lord Jesus, I pray for those
who will be unhappy today:
For parents who have no food
to cook for their children;
for parents who cannot earn
enough money for their families;
for children who are sick or frightened;
and for those who are alone
and without people to love them.

A busy day

Thank you, God, for the daytime
when I can be awake and busy.
Thank you for all there is
for me to do today:
new things to find out,
friends and games to play with.
Thank you for the sun
that gives us warmth and light
to see by.

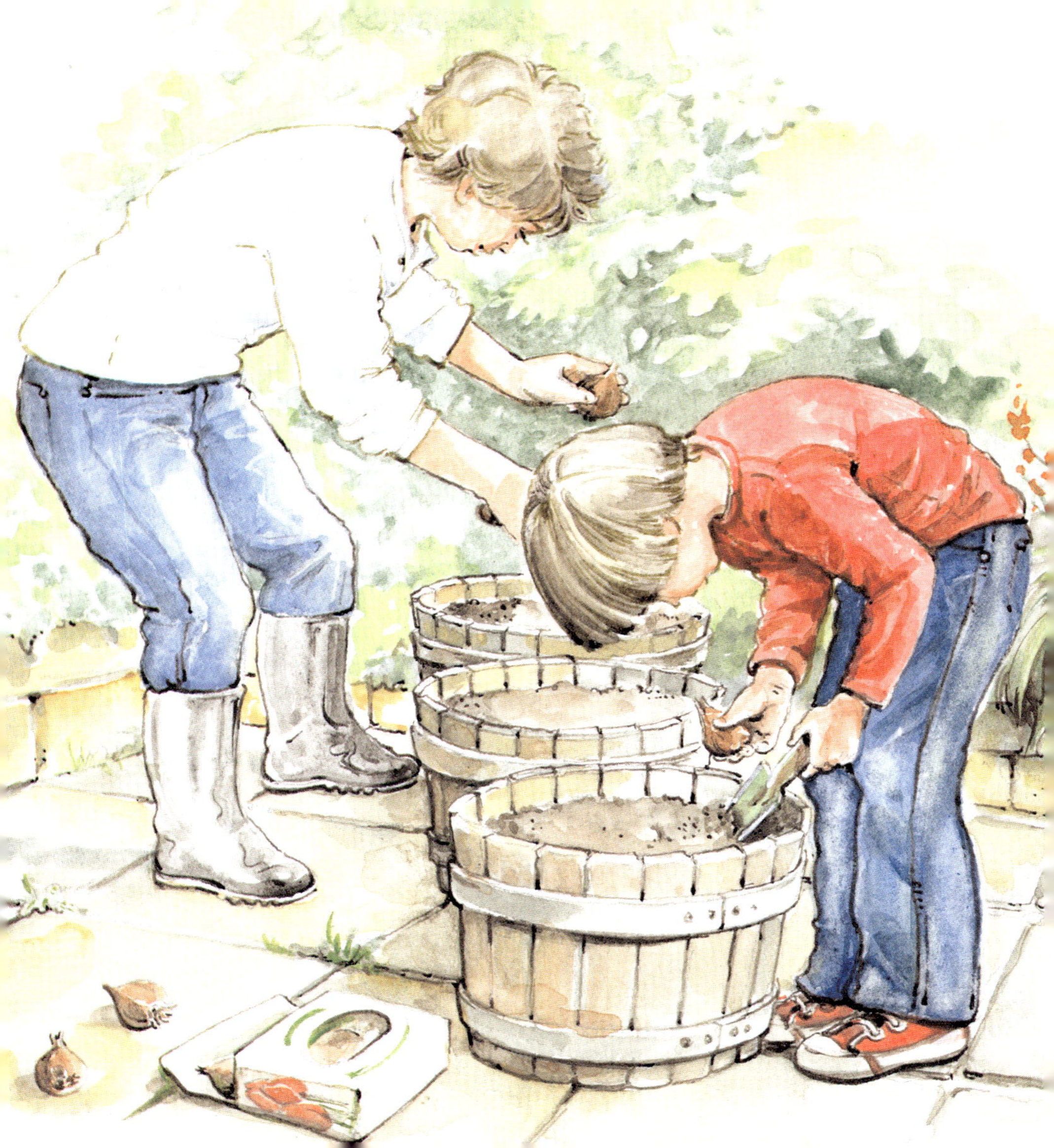

For animals

Dear Father, hear and bless
Thy beasts and singing birds,
And guard with tenderness,
Small things that have no words.

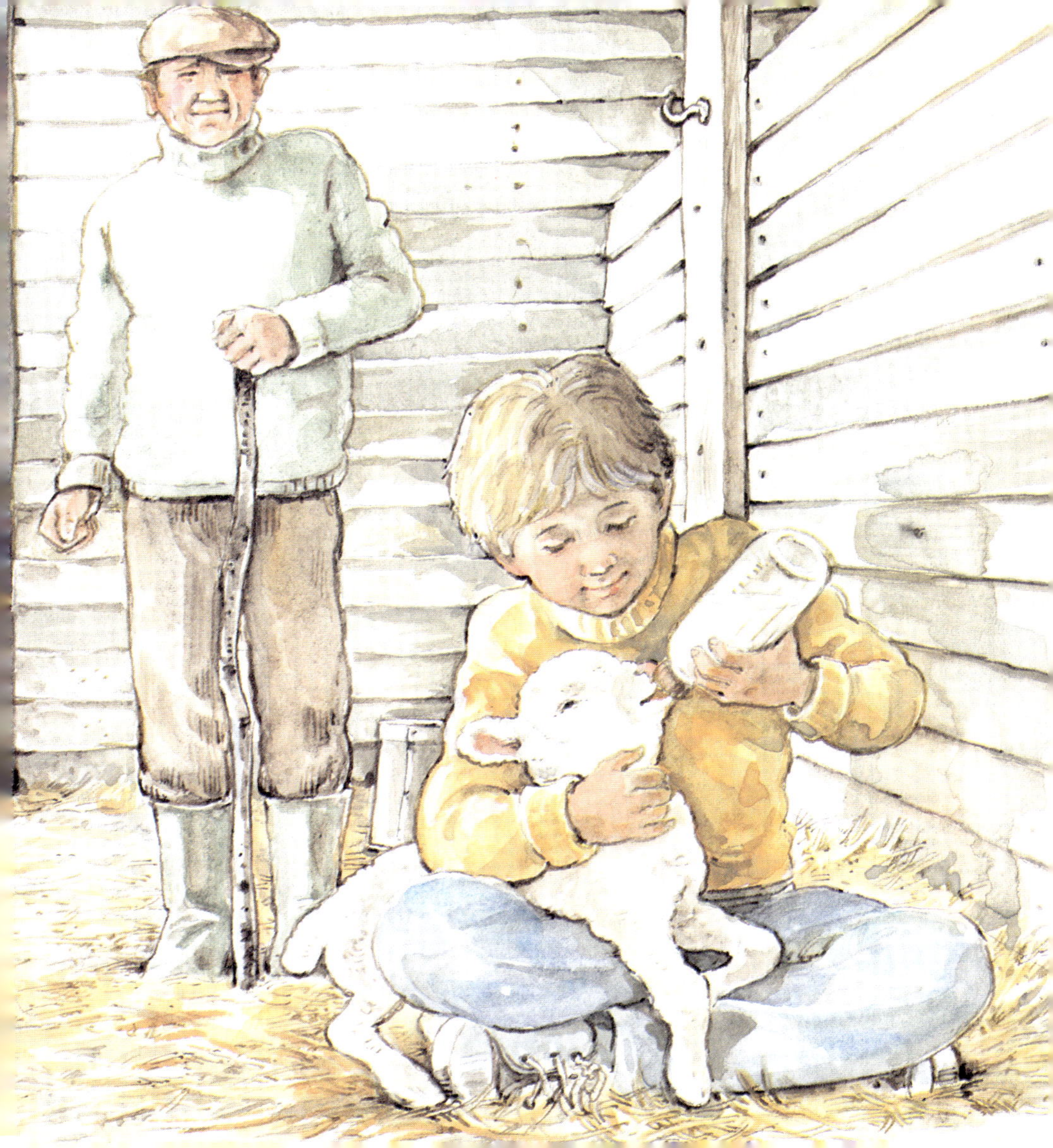

Make me like you

Lord of the loving heart,
May mine be loving too.
Lord of the gentle hands,
May mine be gentle too.
Lord of the willing feet,
May mine be willing too.
So may I grow more like thee
In all I say and do.

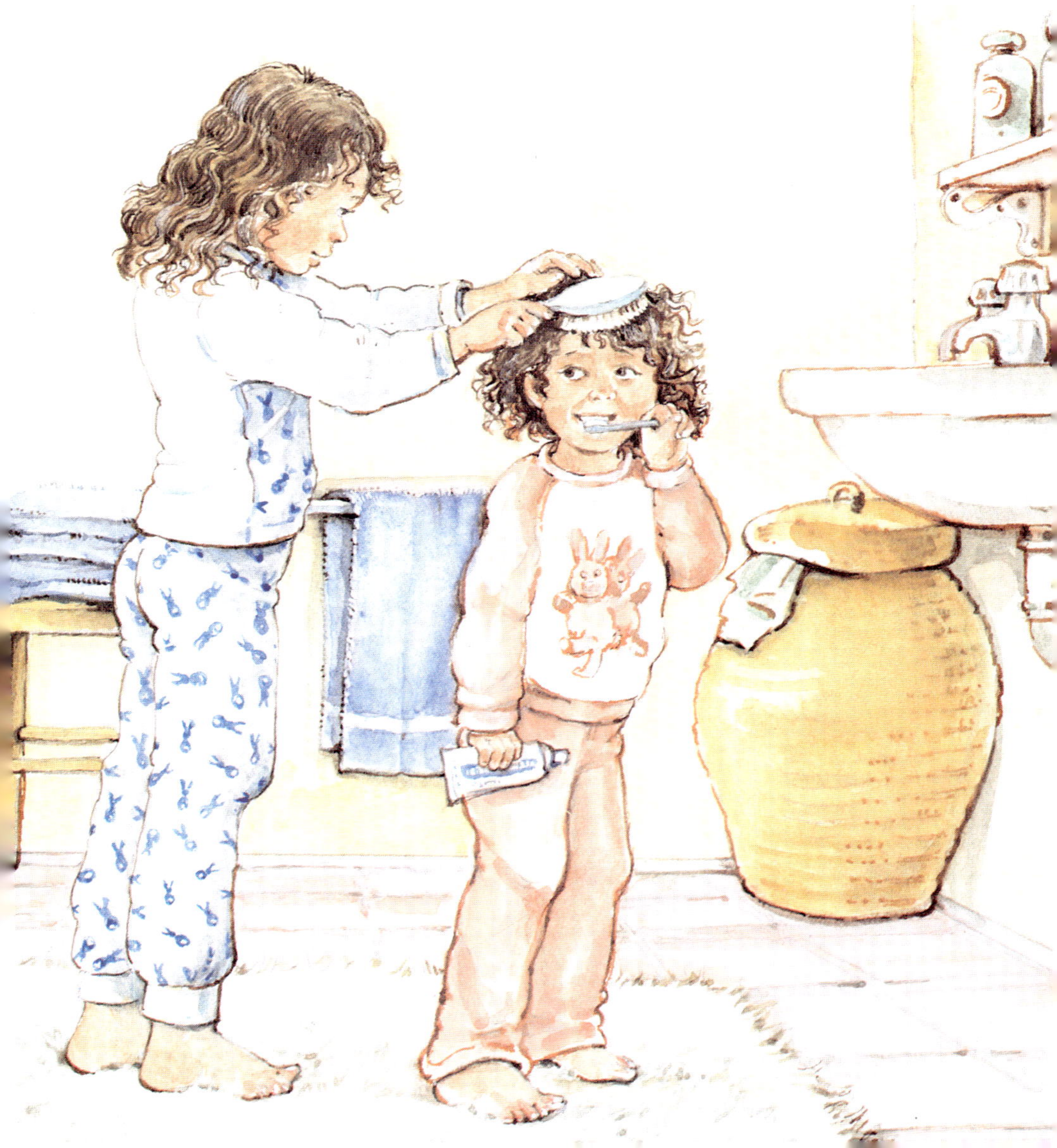

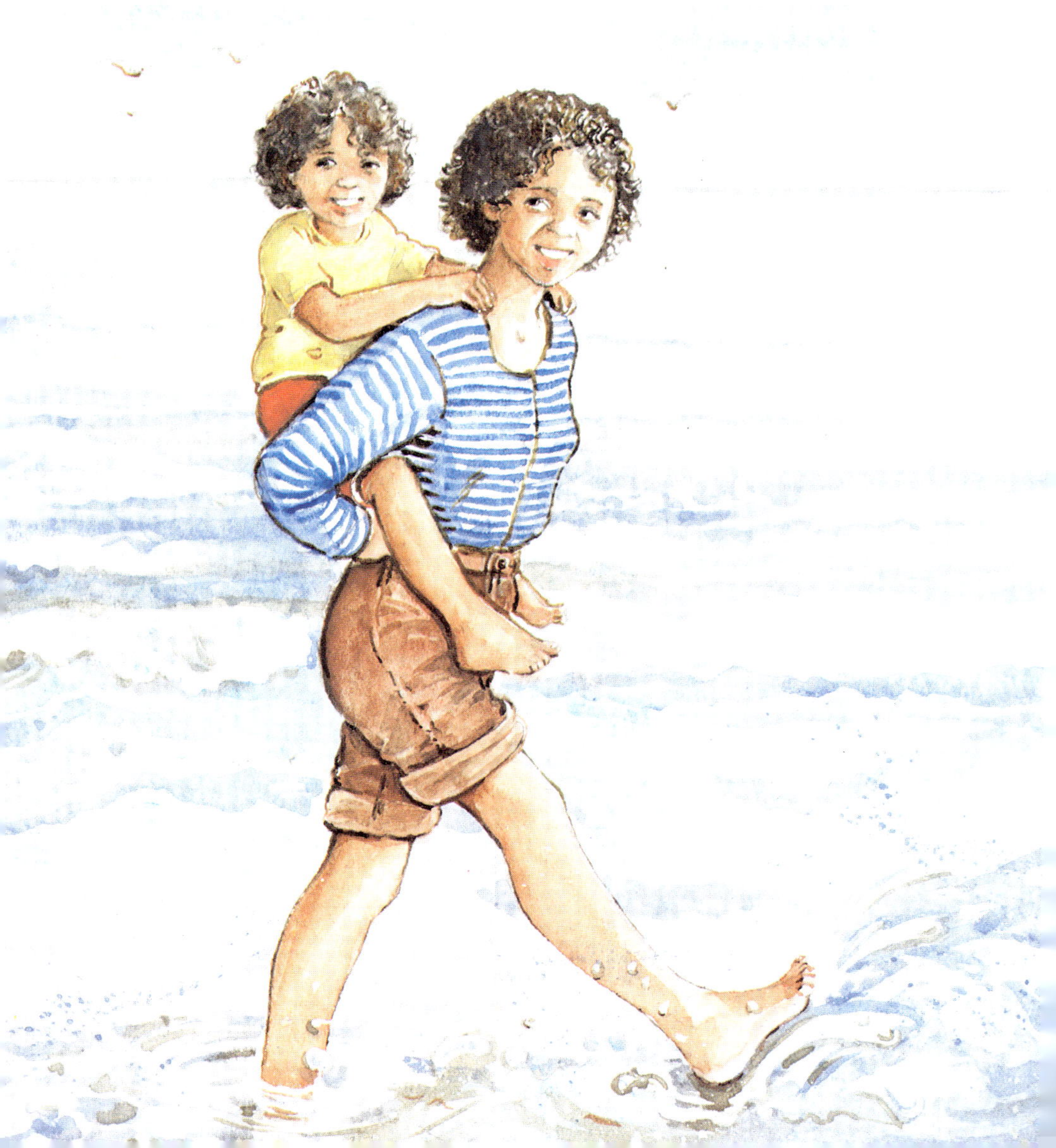

You love us

Thank you, Lord Jesus,
that you love us the same today
as yesterday.

Compilation copyright © 1993 Lion Publishing
Illustrations copyright © 1993 Maureen Bradley

Published by
Lion Publishing plc
Sandy Lane West, Oxford, England
ISBN 0 7459 2840 4 (casebound)
ISBN 0 7459 2638 X (paperback)
Albatross Books Pty Ltd
PO Box 320, Sutherland, NSW 2232, Australia
ISBN 0 7324 0770 2 (casebound)
ISBN 0 7324 0641 2 (paperback)

First edition 1978
This revised edition 1993

10 9 8 7 6 5 4 3 2 1

All rights reserved

Acknowledgments
We thank those who have given us permission to include
prayers in this book and apologize for any copyright omissions.
Cassell plc: from *The Infant Teacher's Prayer Book*
by D.M. Prescott, (Blandford Press), 'Thank you, God, for this new day';
Scripture Union: from *Let's Talk to God* by Zinnia Bryan,
'Thank you, Lord Jesus, that you love us', 'Lord Jesus, I pray for those...'
and 'Thank you, God, for the daytime'.

A catalogue record for this book is available
from the British Library

Printed and bound in Slovenia

6987